By Laura Williams
Translated by Akosua Boateng

© 2022 Williams Books
1 rue de l'église, 91430 Igny
Dépôt légal : Décembre 2022
ISBN 978-2-494614-21-5
Imprimé à la demande par Amazon
Loi n° 49-956 du 16 juillet 1949 sur les publications destinées à la jeunesse

ɔtwe

antelope

apan

bat

osisire

bear

nsonkuronsuo

bedbug

wowa

bee

ɛkoɔ

buffalo

afranfrantɔ
butterfly

yoma
camel

ɔkra

cat

abosomakotrɛ

chameleon

akokɔba

chick

akokɔ

chicken

ntɛfrɛ
cockroach

nantwie
cow

akatakyire

cricket

dɛnkyɛm

crocodile

ɔkraman
dog

afunumpɔnkɔ
donkey

dabodabo

duck

sonsono

earthworm

ɔsono

elephant

mpataa

fish

Ahurii

fly

sakraman

fox

apɔnkyereni
frog

adowa
gazelle

sɔhori

giraffe

apɔnkye

goat

nsu-dokodoko

goose

susono

hipopotamus

poŋkɔ

horse

pataku

hyena

gyata

lion

kotrɛ

lizard

akisi

mole

ahweaa

mongoose

adoe

monkey

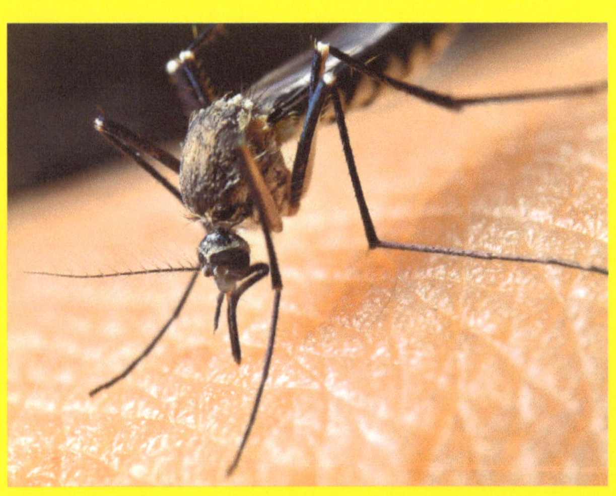

ntomtom

mosquito

akura

mouse

ako

parrot

prɛko

pig

aborɔnoma

pigeon

adanko

rabbit

akokɔnini

rooster

odwan

sheep

nwa

snail

ɔwɔ

snake

ananse

spider

wowa

wasp

afunumu

zebra

Thank you

Thank you for purchasing "Twi-English Words for Toddlers"! Your support means a lot to me, and I hope you and your child enjoy these books.

If you have a moment, I would greatly appreciate it if you could leave a review on Amazon. Your feedback will help me improve future editions of the series and create more resources for bilingual children.

Thank you again for your support. You can access the reviews on Amazon by scanning the QR code below or by visiting the link below:

https://www.amazon.com/review/create-review?&asin=249461421X

Thank you for helping me continue my work as a language teacher and translator. Your support is greatly appreciated!

In the same collection

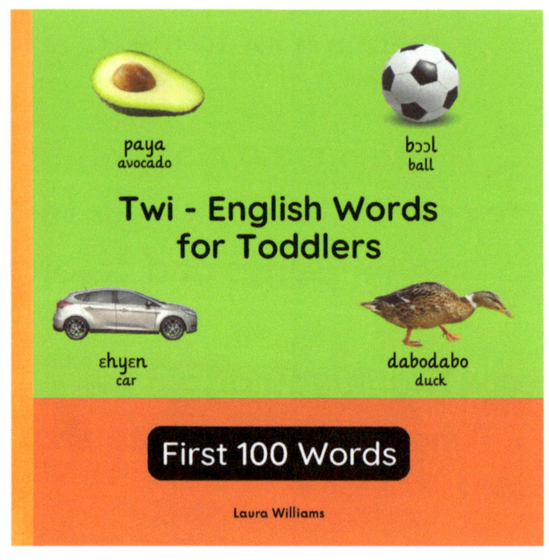

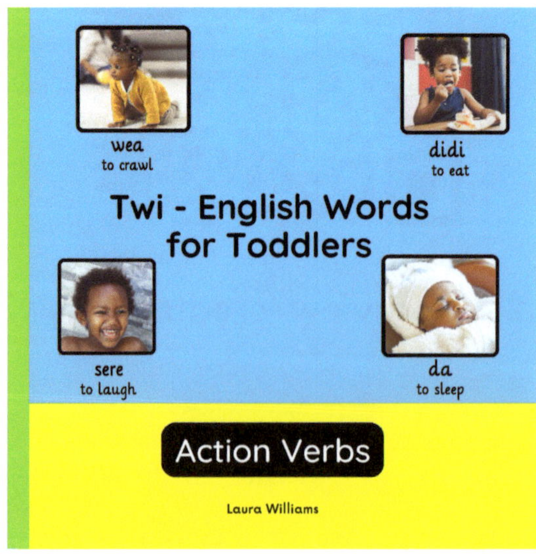

www.ingramcontent.com/pod-product-compliance
Lightning Source LLC
LaVergne TN
LVHW071703180726
843512LV00002B/538